DANGER: MEMORY!

BY ARTHUR MILLER

PLAYS

All My Sons   Death of a Salesman
An Enemy of the People *(adaptation of the play by Ibsen)*
The Crucible
A View from the Bridge *(one-act version, with* A Memory of Two Mondays*)*
A View from the Bridge *(two-act version)*
After the Fall   Incident at Vichy   The Price
The Creation of the World and Other Business

SCREENPLAYS

The Misfits
Playing for Time

NOVEL

Focus

STORIES

I Don't Need You Any More

REPORTAGE

Situation Normal

FOR CHILDREN

Jane's Blanket

WITH INGE MORATH

In Russia
In the Country
Chinese Encounters
Salesman in Beijing

COLLECTIONS

Arthur Miller's Collected Plays *(Volumes I and II)*
The Portable Arthur Miller
The Theater Essays of Arthur Miller *(edited by Robert Martin)*

CRITICAL LIBRARY EDITIONS

Death of a Salesman *(edited by Gerald Weales)*
The Crucible *(edited by Gerald Weales)*

ARTHUR MILLER

Danger: Memory!

TWO PLAYS

I CAN'T REMEMBER ANYTHING

CLARA

GROVE PRESS, INC., New York

DANGER: MEMORY! Copyright © 1986 by Arthur Miller

All rights reserved

No part of this book may be reproduced, stored in a retrieval system, or transmitted in any form, or by any means, including mechanical, electronic, photocopying, recording or otherwise, without prior written permission of the publisher.

Published by Grove Press, Inc.
920 Broadway
New York, N.Y. 10010

Library of Congress Cataloging-in-Publication Data

Miller, Arthur, 1915-
      Danger: Memory!

      I. Title.
PS3525.I5156D28 1987   812'.52   86-29402
ISBN 0-394-56102-3
ISBN 0-394-62353-3 (pbk.)

Designed by Sidney Feinberg

Manufactured in the United States of America
First Edition 1987

10 9 8 7 6 5 4 3 2 1

CONTENTS

I CAN'T REMEMBER ANYTHING

The time is now.

LEO's *living room–kitchen in a nondescript little wooden house on a country back road. A woodburning stove near a handmade plywood dining and drawing table; some canvas folding chairs, one of them repaired with needle and thread; a wicker chair; a couple of short benches; a well-worn modern chair and a lumpy couch— in short, a bachelor's heaven. A couple of fine, dusty landscapes on one wall as well as tacked-up photos and a few drunken line drawings of dead friends.*

At the big table LEO *is carefully lettering with a marker pen on a piece of cardboard, a newspaper open at his elbow. There are a few patches on his denim shirt and his pants are almost nothing but patches. They are his resistance to commercialism in the last quarter of the twentieth century. He has a stubborn little face.*

LEONORA *enters through the front door; she is a large woman who opens her long, many-colored woolen shawl and shakes it out as she sits in a chair not far from him, giving a little cough and swallowing a few times and catching her breath. Now she turns to him. Her speech is New England with a European aristocratic coloration of which, however, she is not aware.*

LEONORA: Well. You might at least look up.

LEO: I saw you.

LEONORA: Well, that's a greeting, isn't it. "I saw you."

LEO: I've got chicken again.

LEONORA: I don't care, everything tastes the same to me anyway. May I have my colored water?

LEO: It's over there.

LEONORA: Thank you. *(She goes, pours some bourbon, holds up the glass, adds a bit more.)*

LEO: You always have to pour it twice.

LEONORA: Because I have to see whether it's enough or too much.

LEO: But it's never too much, it's always too little.

LEONORA *(taking a pitcher and holding it in her hand):* May I have some water?

LEO: There's some in there.

LEONORA: I see that. May I have it?

LEO: You certainly may. *(Finishes his drawing, inspects it, sets it aside. Takes a pencil and starts on a crossword puzzle.)* I see you bashed in your new car.

LEONORA: It's what I said the last time; they are placing these light poles too close to the road.

LEO: The light poles are the same distance they have always been.

LEONORA: Well, they're not, but there's no use arguing about it.

LEO: Maybe you ought to forget about driving under certain conditions.

LEONORA *(sits some distance from him, facing front):* There's simply no use talking to you.

LEO: Not about the distance of light poles to the road there isn't.

LEONORA *(takes a thin package out of her enormous bag):* I got this in the mail this morning; it's from Lawrence.

LEO: It might be one thing if you could be sure to kill yourself. But you're liable to end up crippled or blind or killing somebody else, then what?

LEONORA: Oh, what's the use? *(Sips; a deep relaxing sigh, then. . .)*

LEO: Where is Lawrence?

LEONORA *(glancing at the package):* In Sri Lanka, apparently.

LEO: Is he still in that monastery or whatever the hell it is?

LEONORA: It s not a monastery, it's one of those retreats, I think.—But I can never finish reading one of his letters. He just goes on and on and on until I fall asleep. Do you have a knife?

LEO: On the table.

   She gets up, goes to table, picks up knife, starts cutting package open, indicates whiskey bottle.

LEONORA: You know you're almost out.

LEO: I know, but I couldn't get to town today. Isn't there enough for you?

LEONORA: What about you?

LEO: I haven't touched whiskey in at least a year, since I got my arthritis. Haven't you noticed?

LEONORA: I was just trying to be polite.

LEO: That bottle was full day before yesterday . . . just to remind you.

LEONORA: You've had guests?

LEO (*pointedly*): No, just you.

LEONORA: Well, what's the difference?

LEO: By the way, if you come in here one night and I'm dead, I want you to call Yale–New Haven Hospital and not this . . . whatever you call him . . . mortician what's-his-name in town.

LEONORA: What good is a hospital if you're dead, for God's sake?

LEO: I just finished making arrangements for them to take my organs.

LEONORA: Really!

LEO: For research. So call Yale–New Haven. This mortician here used to have a Nixon bumper sticker.

LEONORA: What do they expect to find from *your* organs?

LEO: Why?—My organs aren't good enough?

LEONORA: But I should imagine they would want people with some interesting disease. All you've got is arthritis. Aside from that, you'll probably die in perfect health.

LEO: Well, I might get something.

LEONORA: Where, for heaven's sake? You never go anywhere but the post office or the grocery store.

LEO: I go to the gas station.

LEONORA: The gas station! What do you expect to pick up at the gas station?

LEO: I don't know. Gas disease.

LEONORA *(laughing):* Gas disease!

LEO: This is another one of those conversations.

LEONORA: Well, I certainly didn't start it.

LEO *(showing her his newly drawn sign in block letters):* This is Yale–New Haven, see? I'm going to tack this number over the phone.

LEONORA: But I'll certainly be dead before you.

LEO: In case you're not dead and you walk in and there I am with my eyes crossed and my tongue hanging out.

LEONORA *(grimacing):* Oh, stop that, for God's sake.

LEO: Well, that's how you look when you have a stroke.

Returns to his newspaper. Pause.

LEONORA: There's nothing in the paper, is there?

LEO: Yes, a few things.

LEONORA: Well, don't tell it to me, it's all too horrible.

LEO: I wasn't going to tell it to you. *(Pause)* You want rice?

LEONORA: I hate rice. *(He returns to his paper.)* Why are you being so difficult, Leo?

LEO: Me? I'm the one who invited you to have rice, for Christ's sake.

LEONORA: I can't for the life of me figure out why I haven't died.

LEO: Well, maybe it'll come to you.

LEONORA: I used to believe, as a girl—I mean, we were taught to believe—that everything has its purpose. You know what I'm referring to.

LEO: My mother was the only atheist in Youngstown, Ohio; she never talked about things having purposes.

LEONORA: Well, in New England you tended to believe those things!—But what purpose have I got? I am totally useless, to myself, my children, my grandchildren, and the one or two people I suppose I can call my friends who aren't dead . . .

LEO: Then why don't you stop being useless?

LEONORA: How can I stop being useless, for God's sake? If a person is useless, she is *useless*.

LEO: Then do something.—Why don't you take up the piano again?

LEONORA: The piano!

LEO: Oh, come on now, for Christ's sake, you used to play Mozart and Chopin and all that stuff. You can't tell me you don't remember playing the piano, Leonora.

LEONORA (*without admission or denial*): I don't know where I'd ever begin a thing like that.

LEO: Well, the accordion, then.

LEONORA: *What?* I certainly never in my life played the *accordion.*

LEO: Except with thirty or forty people dancing on the grass, and everybody pissed to the gills, and Frederick banging on a soup pot, and a big salami tied between his legs.

LEONORA: Really? *(A sudden laugh)* A salami?

LEO: Sure, and a pair of oranges. Waving it around at the women.

LEONORA *(stares):* Sometimes . . . I *think* I remember something, but then I wonder if I just imagined it. My whole life often seems imaginary. It's very strange.

LEO: I know something you could kill time with.

LEONORA: There is nothing. I don't even have the concentration to read anymore. Sometimes I wonder if *I'm* imaginary.

LEO: Why don't you try to get people to donate their organs to Yale–New Haven? You could just sit at home with the phone book and make calls.

LEONORA: You mean I'm to telephone perfect strangers and ask them for their organs?

LEO: Well, it's important; they really need organs.

LEONORA: Where do you *get* these ideas?

LEO: I tell you, I just wish I had your health.

LEONORA: Something's burning.

LEO: Christ, it's the rice! *(Struggles to get up.)*

LEONORA: May I . . . ?

LEO *(waving at her):* Yes! Take it off the stove!

> *She hurries to a point, returns with a pot into which she is looking.*

LEONORA: It looks terrible. You can't eat this.

LEO: Well, I was just using it up. I have salad, it'll be enough.

LEONORA: You only have one plate out.

LEO: Oh? I must have got distracted. I think somebody phoned when I was setting the table.—Who the hell was that, now . . . ?

LEONORA: Perhaps you don't want me to dinner.

LEO: Oh, get a plate, will you? They're right up there in the cabinet.

LEONORA: Good heavens, after all these years I know where the plates are. *(She goes, brings down a plate, knife and fork, and napkin.)*

LEO: I'm having some bread; *you* don't want any, though.

LEONORA: Bread! I haven't eaten bread in a decade.

LEO: You ate some last week . . . that that girl brought me from the nature store.

LEONORA *(stops moving):* I can't remember anything.

LEO: Well, you did. You ate three slices.

LEONORA: I can't have eaten three slices of *bread.*

LEO: You did, though.

LEONORA: I simply cannot remember anything at all.

They are seated at their plates facing each other, and he has served the chicken and they eat. He picks up his pencil and enters a word in the puzzle as he eats.

LEONORA: Oh! Do you mean that young girl with the braids?

LEO *(preoccupied):* Uh-huh.

LEONORA: The one with the lisp.—She's quite pretty.

LEO: Oh, she's some doll.

LEONORA: "Doll!"—I will never understand your attraction for these women when you really don't like women at all.

LEO: I like women. I just don't like dumb women.

LEONORA: Oh, is she clever?

LEO: She's writing a master's thesis on Recurrence. That's a mathematical principle.

LEONORA *(doesn't know what to say):* Well!

LEO: Yes. But you couldn't understand anything like that.— You can talk to that girl about something.

LEONORA: I don't recall you being so intellectually particular in the old days.

LEO: I used to drink more in the old days.

LEONORA: Oh, I see; and now that you can't drink you discuss mathematics.

LEO: Who was the President of France when the War started?

LEONORA: Good God, how should I know?

LEO: Well, you were living there then, weren't you?

LEONORA: Yes, but nobody *ever* knows who the President of France is.

LEO: Well, you wouldn't have known anyway.

LEONORA *(slamming her fork down):* I would certainly have known if it was of any importance.

LEO: No you wouldn't.

LEONORA *(throws her napkin straight at him, speechless with anger. Pause. He goes on with the crossword):* May I have my napkin?

LEO *(returning the napkin to her):* I think it begins with a P.

LEONORA: I hate crossword puzzles. They do nothing but add triviality to the boredom of existence.—"President of France"! Before the War no one *cared* who the President was. It's not like being the President of the United States.

LEO: Everybody knows that, for Christ's sake.

LEONORA: You don't. You don't know anything about France.

LEO: Could it be Poincaire?

LEONORA: "Pwancare"! It's Poincaré.

LEO: Well, Pwancaray.

LEONORA: I believe Poincaré was Prime Minister at some point, but not President. Why do you ask me questions like that? I can't remember anything political. *(Making a face)* Will they take out your brain too?

LEO: I guess so. For sweetbreads.

LEONORA (*screwing up her face*): Why do you *say* things like that!

LEO: And my liver with onions.

She laughs painfully, and then they both eat in silence.

LEONORA: This is really quite good. Is that thyme?

LEO: Rosemary.

LEONORA: I mean rosemary. God, I simply can't keep anything straight.

LEO: You used to use a lot of rosemary.

LEONORA: Did I?

LEO: On gigot. You had a wonderful touch with any kind of lamb, you always had it nice and pink, with just enough well-done at the ends; and the best bread I think I ever ate.

LEONORA: Really!

LEO: You don't remember Frederick holding the bread to his chest, and that way he had of pulling the knife across it, and handing it out piece by piece to people at the table?

Slight pause.

LEONORA: Well, what difference does it make?

LEO: I don't know, it's just a damn shame to forget all that. Your lamb always had absolutely clear pink juice, like rosé wine. And the way you did the string beans, just exactly medium hard. Those were some great dinners.

LEONORA: Were they?

LEO: Yes.

LEONORA: Well, I'm glad you enjoyed them. To me—when I do think of anything like that—it's like some page in a book I once read. Don't you often forget what you've read in a book? What earthly difference does it make?

LEO: But it's not a book, it's your life, kiddo.

LEONORA: Yes, well . . . so what? Look at these millions of people starving to death all over the place, does anyone remember them? Why should I remember myself any more than I remember them?

LEO: Well, it's not the same.

LEONORA: Naturally. That's because you come from central Ohio.

LEO: What the hell's that got to do with it?

LEONORA: In central Ohio everything always turns out for the best.

LEO: Youngstown doesn't, for your information, happen to be in central Ohio.

LEONORA: Well, it might as well be.

LEO: Well, I have work to do tonight.

LEONORA: I won't stay, I'll just sit here for a bit and look out the window. Is that all right?

LEO: Sure.

> *Gets with difficulty to his feet, picks up plates . . .*

LEONORA: Here, let me . . .

LEO *(a command)*: I'll do it! *(He shuffles to the sink as she sits staring front.)* What'd Lawrence send?

LEONORA: Oh!

She had forgotten and reaches to the table and the package, from which she takes a record.

LEO: Another record? Oh, Christ.

LEONORA *(uncertain):* He never sent me a record before.

LEO: Sure he did, about three years ago, that goddam Indian music, it was horrible.

LEONORA: Yes, I remember now . . . It was wonderful for a certain mood.

LEO: Sounded like a bunch of cats locked in a toilet.

LEONORA: What do you know about music, for heaven's sake? *(She finds a note with the record.)* I don't have my glasses. *(Hands him the note.)*

LEO *(reads):* "Dear Mother. This one is quite different. Let me know how you like it. My group has been invited to play in New Delhi, isn't that terrific? Love, Lawrence."

LEONORA: Well!—That's short and sweet, isn't it? After three years, did you say?

LEO: Wait, there's a P.S. "P.S. Moira and I have decided to separate, you'll be glad to hear."

LEONORA: Moira? Who is Moira? *(She stares ahead tensely, struggling to remember.)*

LEO: Sounds like somebody he married. *(He hands back the note. Her eyes moisten with tears which she blinks away, looking at the record.)* I hope you're not going to play that here.

LEONORA: *(an outcry):* I have no intention of playing it here . . . or anywhere, since my machine has been broken for a least five or six years!—When did it all begin getting so vile, do you know? *(He sits at table again and picks up a pencil, poring over some diagrams.)* Are you working at something?

LEO: I promised my friend Bokum I would check out some of his calculations that he made for the new bridge in town.

LEONORA: I didn't even know there was an *old* bridge.

LEO: Across the river; you drive over it half a dozen times a week.

LEONORA: Oh, that one!—Strange, I never think of that as a bridge.

LEO: What do you think of it as?

LEONORA: I don't know . . . just the road. Are you going to rebuild it?

LEO: I'm not doing anything, just checking out Bokum's numbers. *(Opening a file folder)* But everything keeps slipping out of my head. I could do this stuff in twenty minutes and now I can't calculate worth a damn.

LEONORA: Well, now you know what I mean . . .

LEO: That was one thing I admired about Frederick, he never once slowed down mentally.

LEONORA: Didn't he?

LEO: For Christ's sake, you remember whether he slowed down mentally, don't you?

LEONORA: Well, I'm sorry if it irritates you!

LEO: It doesn't "irritate" me, I just don't think you ought to be forgetting that, that's all.—The man was sharp as a tack to his last minute!

LEONORA: You know, I could criticize you too, if I wished to.

LEO: Well, go ahead!

LEONORA: I wouldn't bother. *(Pause)* By the way, I am never going back to your dentist.

LEO: Neither am I. I'm sorry I recommended him.

LEONORA: What gets into you? You are forever sending me to doctors and dentists who are completely incompetent. That man nearly killed me with his drill. Why do you do that?

LEO: I don't know, he seemed okay for a while there.

LEONORA: It was the same thing with that awful plumber. And that idiotic man who fixed the roof and left me in a downpour. I think there's something the matter with you; you get these infatuations with an individual and just when you've got everybody going to them you stop going.

LEO: He just seemed like a nice guy; I don't know.

LEONORA: He seriously wanted to pull out all my teeth.

LEO: Did he? Son of a bitch.

LEONORA: Well, he actually pulled all yours, didn't he? *(She silently swallows a drink.)*

LEO: Well . . . not *all*.

LEONORA: But all the front ones.

LEO: He didn't like my gums.

LEONORA: And you allowed him to pull out all your front teeth?

LEO *(defensively angry):* Well, he seemed okay! I liked him!

LEONORA: Yes, you certainly did. *(She looks at her glass.)* May I have another? *(He nods, studying his puzzle. She goes and pours.)* All it is is a little color for conviviality. *(She returns to her chair, sits.)* I saw the most beautiful young deer today. Near the waterfall, so she couldn't hear me until my car was right next to her. She turned to me and there was such a look of surprise! I felt ashamed. Imagine how frightening we must be to them! And how we must stink, when they feed on nothing but grass and green things. And we full of dead chickens and rotting cow meat . . . *(She drinks. He does his puzzle.)*

LEO: You know it's Frederick's birthday tomorrow.

LEONORA *(with a faint guilt in her eye)*: Tomorrow? *(He gives her an impatient, nearly angry look.)* Why do you look at me like that? I simply didn't think of it. *(With defiance)* I never think of anything. I just drive around the country-side and look at the trees, I don't see what's wrong with that. I love the trees; they are strong and proud and they live a long time, and I love them very much. *(She is filling up, takes a breath to suppress her feelings.)* Everything is so awful, Leo; really and truly this is not the same country.

LEO: You don't have to convince me. I've been a Communist all my life and I still am, I don't care what they say.

LEONORA: I believe you really are, aren't you?—And why not?—You've always given everything you have away. It's your finest trait. But I think . . . were we in Russia once . . . ?

LEO: Sure you were, about twenty years ago . . .

LEONORA: All I remember is that it was all perfectly dread-ful.

LEO: Well, you were rich.

LEONORA: Oh, by the way . . . *(Digging into her large bag, brings out a large handful of unopened envelopes and lays them on the table before him.)* The lawyers say I ought to give away a lot more, would you look at these? I've been meaning to bring them all week.

LEO: Jesus!—They've really got your name down. But I don't know anything about these organizations. Christ, here's the Baptist Mission to Pakistan.

LEONORA: Good God!—There's something there for African Relief, isn't there?

LEO: You sent them something last time, didn't you?

LEONORA: But there are so many of those children. Would five thousand seem too much? I'd like it to matter.

LEO: If that's what you want, go ahead.

LEONORA: Except that I read that some of the money never gets there; it's stolen, they say.

LEO: I don't know what to tell you.

LEONORA: How terrible it is . . . In the old days I never once thought of someone stealing money we donated to . . . like the Spanish Republicans, for instance. Did you?

LEO: Well, people believed in something those days.

LEONORA: But what do they have to *believe?*—It's just common decency. Or is that a stupid thing to say? Tell me honestly—wasn't there something more precious about human life before . . . let's say . . . before the War?

LEO: Maybe. Although not in Ohio. I mean my father died drunk in the entrance of a coal mine—the other guys just

forgot he was in there and they come back next morning
and he'd froze to death, just croaked.

LEONORA: Why do you use that *language?*

LEO: It'll be dark in a few minutes, you're going to have
to drive that car.

LEONORA: I'm perfectly fine. May I have what's left?

LEO: Well . . . if that's what you want, sure.

*He watches her, not approvingly, as she pours the
whiskey and water.*

LEONORA *(sitting):* Have you ever seen that raccoon again?

LEO: Which raccoon?

LEONORA: The one who stole your hamburgers off the outdoor griddle.

LEO *(laughs):* Oh, him! Yeah, he comes by occasionally.—
Although not for a couple of weeks now.

LEONORA: I will never forget your description of how he
tossed the hot hamburger from one paw to another to cool
it off.

LEO *(chuckling):* Oh, yeah . . . *(Mimes tossing a hot hamburger from hand to hand. She guffaws.)*

LEONORA *(through her laughter):* And how did you describe
him?—Like a chef in a fur coat?

LEO: Well, he looked . . . kind of annoyed, y'know? Like a
French chef. Haven't seen him around for quite a while,
though. Probably got shot by now.

Pause. She sips, staring out the window.

LEONORA: Why don't they leave those poor animals alone?

LEO: Well, for one thing, the deer are ruining the apple trees.

LEONORA: Well, maybe that is what they're supposed to be doing. Would you like to be shot because you ate something?

> *He works his crossword puzzle. She sips, stares out the window.*

LEO: It's your birthday too, of course. *(She glances at him. He returns to his puzzle.)* Happy birthday. *(She stares front, a certain distress in her eyes.)* I guess there's no reason not to tell you . . . I still miss him. He was the greatest man I ever met in my life.

LEONORA: Was he?

LEO: Yes, he was. It's over ten years and I don't think a day goes by that I don't hear his laugh or that nasal voice. God, he had common sense.

LEONORA *(after a long sip, and an inhale):* He shouldn't have died first, Leo.

LEO: I know. *(Pause)* Listen: just in case you come in here some night and find me dead, I think he'd have wanted you to . . . live. I'm sure of that, kiddo.

> *Pause.*

LEONORA: We were married just a month over forty-five years; that's a very long time, Leo.

LEO: But even so . . .

LEONORA: One can't just skip off and start over again.

LEO: You're twelve years older than me and you've got more life in you than I have. Chrissake, you hardly look sixty-five, if that; you might have ten years to go yet . . .

LEONORA: Oh, God help me.

LEO: How about taking a trip somewhere, maybe find somebody to go along with you?

LEONORA: Everybody is dead, don't you realize that? Everybody except you.

LEO: It doesn't seem possible . . . All those hundreds of people that used to be at your parties . . . Three days later there'd still be people sleeping it off in the flower beds or out in the cars.

LEONORA: All dead.

LEO: Well, they can't *all* be . . .

LEONORA: . . . For God's sake, Leo, the last party must have been at least fifteen years ago! There's something the matter with you. You are not growing old, or something.

LEO: How about Asia? You've never been to Asia.

LEONORA: You're getting worse than I am. When Frederick did that Ganges bridge, and we were six months with the Maharajah . . . ?

LEO: Maybe you could visit him?

LEONORA: Good heavens, he was nearly seventy twenty years ago . . . Anyway, I hated it there; all that bowing and scraping, and those poor elephants. And everyone telling you nothing but lies.—And besides, those people were Frederick's friends, not mine. All our friends were.

LEO: Even so, Frederick was absolutely nuts about you, Leonora, you can't ever forget that.

LEONORA: Of course. I'm not talking about *that. (Pause. A smile grows on her face.)* The very first time we met . . .

LEO: . . . On a train, wasn't it?

LEONORA: Of course . . . to California for one of his bridges there. And he found my mother alone in the dining car and said, "Your daughter has the finest backside I have ever seen."

LEO: Ha! She wasn't scandalized?

LEONORA: Why? It's a complimentary thing to say, isn't it? Besides, she was still headmistress of the Boston College for Women.

LEO: So?

LEONORA: Well, she had plenty of means of comparison. *(Laughs her high, hawking laugh.)*

LEO: See now?—You remembered all that.

LEONORA *(a tension rises in her, which she suppresses)*: Well, that was so long ago it hardly matters. *(Nearly blushing)* I want to ask you something personal, may I? *(He turns to her, waiting.)* Well, may I?

LEO: What?

LEONORA: Why do you pretend that you aren't discouraged?

LEO *(surprised by this)*: . . . Well, I'm not as down on everything as *you* are, but . . .

LEONORA *(her anxiety intensifying)*: But why can't you just admit that it's all nothing? You *know* it's nothing, Leo.

LEO *(stalling)*: What's nothing?

LEONORA: Why, our lives, the whole damned thing.—That's what is so irritating, you simply refuse to . . . to . . . *(A*

new idea) I mean you go on and on reading that stupid
newspaper with the same vileness every day, the same
brutality, the same lies . . .

LEO: Well, I like to know what's happening.

LEONORA: But nothing is "happening"! Excepting that it
keeps getting worse and more brutal and more vile . . .

LEO: What the hell are you getting so angry about if I read
a newspaper?

LEONORA: Because after thirty or forty or whatever goddamned awful number of years it is, you are still a sort of
strangeness to me. I ought to know you by now, oughtn't
I? Well, I don't. I don't know you, Leo!

*He is mystified but impressed with the depth of her feel-
ing, and wondering what she is trying to say to him.
He watches her profile.*

LEO: Well, what would you like to know?

LEONORA: Every evening I feel this same condescension from
you, when you know perfectly well that it is all contin-
ually getting worse.

LEO: Listen, I'm depressed too . . .

LEONORA: No, you are not depressed, you just try to *sound*
depressed. But in the back of your mind you are still se-
cretly expecting heaven-knows-what incredible improve-
ment just over the horizon.

LEO: I still don't understand what you're trying to . . .

LEONORA: This country is being ruined by greed and men-
dacity and narrow-minded ignorance, and you go right on
thinking there is hope somewhere. And yet you really don't,
do you?—but you refuse to admit that you have lost your

hope. That's exactly right, yes—it's this goddamned hopefulness when there is no hope—that is why you are so frustrating to sit with!

LEO *(he lets her steam for a minute):* The trouble is you don't understand science.

LEONORA: Science! I am asking you for your truthful opinion about your *life!* What has that to do with science, for God's sake?

LEO: Well, I don't think I'm as important as *you* think *you* are.

LEONORA *(caught by a suggestion now):* Ah. That's interesting.

LEO: I never accomplished anything much except . . .

LEONORA: Why?—You helped Frederick immensely for . . . more than twenty years, wasn't it? And before that you taught so many students . . .

LEO: Well, the thing is, I figure I've done what I could do, more or less, and now I'm going back to being a chemical; all we are is a lot of talking nitrogen, you know . . .

LEONORA *(outraged, and laughing):* Talking nitrogen!

LEO: And phosphorus and some other elements . . . about two dollars' worth if you discount inflation. So if you're wondering why you're alive . . . maybe it's because you *are,* that's all, and that's the whole goddam reason. Maybe you're so nervous because you keep looking for some other reason and there isn't any.

   Pause.

LEONORA: It's not that, Leo.

LEO: I know.

LEONORA: What do you know?

LEO: Frederick was your life, and now there's nothing.

LEONORA *(with a wild, furious grin):* So if I told you how unimportant I think I am, I might disappear in thin air, like a speck of dust on the nose of a mouse.

LEO: Okay, well . . . I've got to work.

LEONORA: I don't even remember why we started talking about this.

LEO: That's better than me—I don't even remember what we were talking about.

LEONORA *(laughs, throwing her head back, deep prolonged laughter filled with pain):* . . . Oh, dear, dear . . .

LEO: I've got to get this done.

He bends over his papers.

LEONORA: *(looking at the record in her hand):* Could I play just one minute of it? My machine's really broken.

LEO: Okay, a minute, but that's all.

LEONORA *(puts record on the turntable):* Am I wrong? Didn't you and I dance once?

LEO: Once?

LEONORA: More?

LEO *(shaking his head as though all they did was dance):* Phew!—Okay, forget it.

LEONORA: Oh, of course!

LEO: Christ, there must have been a couple hundred nights when I'd come over and just the three of us would play

records, and Frederick and I would take turns dancing with
you 'cause you'd never get tired . . . and drink a dozen
bottles of wine . . . and he had that fantastic French corkscrew . . .

LEONORA *(as she lowers the tone arm on the record . . .):* I
think I still have that corkscrew . . .

> *Music: A samba beat, but with wild, lacy arpeggios and
> a driving underbeat.*

LEO *(They both listen for a moment. He is pleasantly surprised):* Chrissake, that's nothing but a samba. *(She listens.)* Isn't it? *(He moves his shoulders to the beat.)* Sure,
it's just a plain old-fashion' samba. *(She begins to move to
it. She is remarkably nimble, taking little expert steps . . .
and her sensuality provokes and embarrasses him, making
him laugh tightly . . .)* You dancing, for Christ's sake?

> *She lets herself into the dance fully now, and he lets his
> laughter flower, and, laughing, he struggles to his feet
> and, unable to move more than an inch at a time, he
> swings his shoulders instead, clapping his gnarled hands.
> And she faces him tauntingly, reddening with shyness
> and her flaunting emotions; one moment bent over and
> backing nearly into him, the next, thumbing her nose
> at him, and as the music explodes to its crescendo she
> falls into a chair, breathless, and he collapses into an-
> other and they both sit there laughing, trying to breathe.
> The music ends.*

LEO: Well, that's sure as hell not Indian music. Maybe he
decided to stop wasting his time and start playing human
music.

LEONORA: He does what is in him to do. Just like you. And
everyone else. Until it all comes to an end. . . . Well, thank

you for dinner . . . *(She stands, a bit unsteadily; he turns back to his calculating.)* Shall I come by for breakfast? *(He doesn't reply, staring at the paper.)* Is something wrong?

LEO: I just can't calculate. Phew, this is the worst yet. I used to be able to do these logarithms a-b-c and now . . . it all keeps getting stuck. *(Struggling to his feet)* I think I'll go to bed and get up early. Stay and watch the tube if you like.

LEONORA *(still a bit breathless, throwing her shawl over her shoulders):* Good night, Leo.

LEO: Maybe stay.

LEONORA: Don't be silly, I only have to drive a few hundred yards.

LEO: Well, suit yourself. Be sure you turn your headlights on, it's pitch out there. I don't think there's a moon.

LEONORA: Isn't that the moon?

LEO: That's my outside lamp, for Christ's sake. Listen, maybe better stay here, but I've got to go to sleep and get up with a clear head; I promised Bokum I'd have it tomorrow.

LEONORA: No-no, I'm going.

LEO: Then go, will you? Good night.

LEONORA: Thanks for remembering . . . our birthday. *(She starts for the door.)*

LEO: Leonora? *(She halts.)* We could have a lot more interesting conversations if you'd stop saying you can't remember anything.

LEONORA: Or if you could occasionally learn to accept bad news?

LEO (*waving her off, going toward his bedroom*): Call me when you get home.

LEONORA: It doesn't matter. Good night.

> *He shuffles out as she goes to the door. Once he is gone, she halts. Then goes back to the table and picks up the cardboard sign he had printed with the hospital's number and holds it at arm's length to read it. Puts it down, staring at the air, then goes out. He reappears, shirt off, suspenders hanging down, his nightgown trailing from his hand. Goes to the door and opens it as a motor starts. Headlights cross the window and flash upon him in the doorway and vanish as the car speeds up the road. He leans far out the doorway to watch it going away.*

> *He closes the door, slips the nightgown over his head, sits down painfully, manages to get out of his trousers, then stands and goes to the phone, addressing it.*

LEO: Well, come on, will you?—I've got to go to sleep!

> *Phone remaining silent, he goes to table, takes the cardboard sign and with a couple of pushpins fastens it to the wall over the phone. It reads, "Yale–N. Haven 771-8515." The phone rings.*

LEO (*into phone*): Okay. Yeah, good night, good night. (*Hangs up and, shuffling to his bedroom, with his pants trailing from his hand, he shakes his head . . .*) Jesus . . . !

C U R T A I N

CLARA

Living room of CLARA KROLL's apartment-office. All the action is confined to a small lighted area downstage. Beyond it are suggestions of the room, which in a few feet are swiftly lost in the surrounding darkness.

A couple of MEN are heard quietly talking in what is probably an adjoining room, then silence.

A MAN is lying on the floor with one arm resting over his eyes. He is in a suit and topcoat and his overturned hat lies nearby. He is ALBERT KROLL.

DETECTIVE LIEUTENANT FINE enters from the darkness carrying a file drawer, which he sets on a small table beside a chair, and sits.

The reflection of a camera flash illuminates the darkness for a second.

Once settled in his chair, FINE glances down at KROLL, then pulls a folder from the file and opens it, removing letter after letter, which he quickly scans. Again little bursts of quiet conversation from the adjoining room, and silence.

A loud saxophone—John Coltrane—splits the air. FINE turns in his chair and shouts upstage.

FINE: Hey! Who's doing that! Shut that off! *(Record stops.)* Tierney? Is that you?

*Out of the darkness upstage, TIERNEY, a young cop, en-
ters, record envelopes under his arm.*

TIERNEY: Sorry, Lieutenant. I happened to touch the but-
ton on the turntable.

FINE: I want Douglas to dust that record for prints, they
may have been playing it.

TIERNEY: It's okay, I didn't touch the record.—She must
have been in the Peace Corps, there's a citation on her
office wall.

FINE *(returning to the file):* I know.

TIERNEY *(starting upstage):* By the way, who's going to feed the
budgie in the kitchen? (FINE *looks up at him.)* That bird in the
cage.

FINE: You want it?

TIERNEY: I mean it's going to die.

FINE: It's okay, steal it. (TIERNEY *turns to leave.)* But nobody has to feed those phonograph records.

A flashbulb in the dimness far upstage.

TIERNEY: I'm lookin', that's all . . . She had quite a collec-
tion here.

FINE: Right. (TIERNEY *exits.* FINE *scans letter after letter. It
is not getting him anywhere. He sits back in the chair, staring ahead.* KROLL *moves his arm.* FINE *turns, looks down at
him.)* How are you coming, Mr. Kroll? (KROLL *is silent.)*
You hearing me now? (KROLL *manages to get up on his
elbows.)* Feeling any better?

EFFECT: *Upstage in darkness an exploding flash illuminates for a subliminal instant in the air over the two*

men a color photo of the bloodied body of a partially stripped woman.

KROLL: I can't understand why I didn't think of it: she may be gone skiing somewhere.

FINE *(A pause. And with a gesture toward upstage . . .):* You've seen her, haven't you?

Now KROLL *sits up completely, staring.*

FINE: You know who I am now.

KROLL: The Lieutenant. (EFFECT: *a color photo of a bloody, wounded hand appears overhead, lasting a millisecond or so.*) Why am I seeing these pictures?

FINE: They're photographing the body. Polaroids.

KROLL: Ah! . . . But why would they be coming through to me?—Oh, it's because there's no rubber in the camera, is that it? (FINE *is silent.*) . . . Except . . . No, that's not right. *(Confused, brows knitted, he stares for a moment.)* Well, one thing anyway—when she gets a look at these shots she'll know what I've been talking about . . . Setting up an office in a neighborhood like this. They always smell of cats.

FINE *(not ungently):* Mr. Kroll, you told me you had a look at her when you walked in, didn't you?

KROLL: That's what I'm talking about. But she has that . . . kind of dedication, you just can't budge her. *(Suddenly laughs.)* "Rubber in the camera!"—Jesus, what an idea! Boy . . . ! *(Shakes his head as he laughs and rubs his forehead.)* Don't mind me, I'll be all right.

FINE: Don't rush; shock can be funny; I've got to wait for the Medical Examiner anyway. Wouldn't you feel better in a chair?

KROLL: In a minute; I don't want heights just yet.

FINE: Take your time. *(Starts to read a letter . . .)*

KROLL: Time did you say?

FINE: One-o-five.

KROLL *(smiles):* . . . Don't you ever look at your watch?

FINE: Don't have to. You know who I am now?

KROLL: Oh, sure. Sorry I mixed you up with Bert, but you're almost the spitting image, even the way you sit with your legs crossed. And the same kind of attitude.

FINE: Well, there are only so many types, you know.

KROLL: Bert and I. I'm going back a ways now, but we were so damned close for years and years. One morning, out of the blue . . . this was after I'd been doing all his landscaping for at least ten years . . . and never a contract—a handshake and that's that. And I show up on this particular Monday morning with my crew and my tractors and he comes out and says, "What're you doing, Albert?" And I says, "We're going to start the grading. . ."—he'd put up these twenty, thirty houses, y'see . . . and he says, "I got somebody else, Albert, I'm sorry." And that was that! *(Laughs.)* Completely out of the blue! Man was practically my best friend. *(Laughs, shakes his head.)*

FINE *(after a pause):* What's the point of that story, Mr. Kroll?

KROLL: . . . I don't know, I guess I'm just talking, it's that you just can't ever let yourself rely on anything staying the way it is . . . *(He suddenly cries out in paroxysms of horror and clamps his hands over his eyes, and continues crying out with great heaves of breath. FINE does not move, watching him as gradually his cries weaken and he goes silent.)*

FINE: It's up to you, but in my experience it's generally better to talk about it. What you can't chase you'd better face or it'll start chasing you, know what I mean? I'd appreciate if we could talk right now, because whoever did this has a big headstart on me and I would like very much to catch up with him.

KROLL: I think she was robbed once before . . .

FINE: No robbery this time . . .

KROLL: No. I remember now, that's right.

FINE: There are two cups on the stove with teabags, and the kettle is melted. There was a fight but no sign of forced entry, and there's still over a hundred dollars in her pocketbook, and the TV and the rest all untouched. It was somebody she was making tea for . . . You with me?

KROLL: Huh?—Yes, making tea for.—Have I called my wife?

FINE: Not to my knowledge. Would you like me to?

KROLL: Oh, no! No, please, I'll . . . I'll do it. *(Takes a breath, looking around.)* Go ahead, I can talk. Someone she was making tea for.

FINE: You're clear about what's happened, right?

KROLL: It . . . starts to slip away now and then, but, yes, I . . .

FINE: Try to hold on to it; Clara's been attacked and murdered.

KROLL: I've no idea. *(Shaking his head)* Funny, I was in the middle of a zoning board meeting . . . last night, I guess—

yeah, last night. And I got this sudden feeling of . . . I felt lonely for her. So I called here when I got home and there was no answer. And this morning Saint Francis hadn't heard from her either.

FINE: She on the staff there? *(Stands, bends over to touch his shoes.)*

KROLL *(nods):* Not that we've been in touch that often but, you know, with this kind of a neighborhood I decided to come down . . . Bad back?

FINE *(straightening up):* Nothing, just psychosomatic. I've been trying to decide whether to retire. My body seems to be voting.

KROLL: What'll you do?

FINE: What they all do—sit looking at the ocean some-where, wondering where my life went.—What was her idea moving into an area like this, do you know?

KROLL: Oh, it goes back a long way with her; she was hardly fifteen, sixteen when she got this job going into back al-leys in Poughkeepsie all hours of the night; teaching these women how to take care of children, nutrition, so on. Just never knew what fear was.

FINE: I notice there's only one lock on the door.

KROLL: I'm surprised there's that one! Even as a child, this great big dog came charging down the street, snarling, snapping, people running into their houses, they thought he was rabid maybe, and there's Clara playing in the front yard with her doll and just holds out her hand . . . *(he holds out his hand)* . . . and that dog stopped in his tracks, quieted right down and just sat.

FINE: Huh! *(Shakes his head.)*

> CLARA *enters out of the darkness holding up a birdcage and extending one finger, crosses and vanishes.*

FINE: Incidentally, her bird is here. You want it?

KROLL: Ah . . . I don't think so. Maybe we could get somebody to . . . ?

FINE: One of the cops wants it.

KROLL: Good. Same thing with that bird . . . always had to have a bird; and lets them out and holds out her finger and they come right back and she pops them into the cage. I don't know where she gets that from . . . You say I haven't called my wife.

FINE: You've been lying there since I came in. How do you feel, you think you could answer a few questions?

KROLL: I simply can't believe it. She loves everybody.

FINE *(glancing about):* It has that atmosphere. She never seems to have been married, is that right?

KROLL: Married? No. *(Seems to change his mind.)* Ah . . . no.

FINE: Something you want to say . . . ?

KROLL: No—no . . . I thought I heard voices.

FINE: There's a man dusting for fingerprints. You're clear now about who I am and where you are, right?

KROLL: . . . And your name again? I'm sorry . . .

FINE: That's all right. Lew Fine.

KROLL: Oh, that's why!—My friend was Bert Fine.

FINE: How old was Clara, by the way?

KROLL: She's . . . let's see . . .

FINE: Was.

KROLL: What?

FINE: She was.

KROLL: Oh. Yes. God. *(Slight pause)* Twenty-eight last July.

> CLARA *enters, closing the door of a cage in which there is now a bird; she pauses behind* KROLL, *and a look of intense love passes over a sublime smile on her face and she moves away in the darkness.*

FINE: Look, Mr. Kroll, if I'm going to get anywhere . . .

KROLL: No—no, please—I'm with you. It's just so unreal to me that I . . .

FINE: I understand, but every minute counts in a thing like this. Now, what can you tell me about Clara? For instance, these files don't indicate any female patients . . .

KROLL: Oh, well, she was mainly interested in prisoner rehabilitation.

FINE: Ah.

KROLL: She worked for three years in Botsford Penitentiary . . . and also Mount Carmel.

FINE: Ah, good—that's good information. And then I suppose she worked with these men after they got out.

KROLL: Oh, yes, helped a lot of them. Had wonderful letters from them. They idolized her.

FINE: I can imagine. You sound very proud of her.

KROLL: Oh, I guess so, I just . . . you just can't help worrying about her, that's all.

FINE: Well, you had reason. Did you kill your daughter, Mister Kroll?

KROLL (*instantly*): What!

FINE: I just wanted you to notice how clean and direct that answer was. Can you feel it? There was no flypaper on that answer. Sorry if I shocked you, but why don't you try to give me clean, direct answers like that, huh?

KROLL: I'm not trying to . . .

FINE: I realize you're all upset . . .

KROLL: Good God, I have to call my wife! Why wouldn't I be upset!

FINE: Okay, okay . . .

KROLL (*almost embarrassed*): It's amazing. The way you say okay, okay . . . that's exactly like Bert.

FINE: Well, there are just so many human types, you know.

KROLL: . . . I just thought of something to ask you, but I'm embarrassed to.

FINE: Go ahead.

KROLL: Well . . . no . . .

FINE: Come on, let's get to know each other.

KROLL: Do you have all your toes?

FINE (*silent for a moment*): No.

KROLL *stares at the floor, shakes his head, lost.*

FINE: Does that depress you?

KROLL: Is it the left foot?

FINE: What's so amazing? After all, we've got interchangeable kidneys, hearts, and a coupla ten years from now we'll all be working for two or three big corporations . . . so your friend and I have missing toes, so what? I don't think I'm anything special, you think you're something special?

KROLL: I can't believe this is happening.

FINE: Why?—He probably lost them in the War, right?

KROLL: That's right. France.

FINE: Well, you realize the number of men lost toes on their left foot in all the wars?

KROLL: . . . You just made me realize something.—I never thought of it this way, but for two or three years before we broke up, he was really turning into a first-class son of a bitch.

FINE (laughs happily): Well, you've learned something tonight, anyway.

KROLL: Oh, yeah . . . He really started cheating his suppliers and nobody could collect on him without threatening to go to court. (Laughs.) I should be glad to have gotten rid of him instead of . . . !

FINE: . . .You've got a real sentimental streak, don't you?

KROLL: Well . . . you like to give people the benefit of the doubt. I mean, by the same token, Bert could turn around and be, you know—warmhearted and generous, and—God!—intelligent . . . ?

FINE: Yeah, and then slit you right up the belly.

KROLL *(looking out, aware . . .):* You know?—In the old days I can't remember people being this complicated.

FINE: Why complicated?

KROLL: You mean . . . ?

FINE: Sure, nothing's changed. I'd like to get back to your daughter, can we?

KROLL: You have children?

FINE *(his smile vanishing):* One . . .

KROLL: . . . Didn't kill himself, did he?

FINE *(nods):* Mmhm.

> KROLL *presses his fingers to his eyes.*

FINE: Nothing to be depressed about; a good number of them did that to themselves during Vietnam, probably hundreds. Our statistics probably crossed, your friend and I, it's bound to happen somewhere on the graph. Same as your daughter, probably. Nine times out of ten she'd have been perfectly okay down here, but she might've said the wrong thing to the wrong guy at the wrong minute, and— *(A gesture)* We're all one step away from a statistic, Albert.—What do you say we get back to it? Why don't you get up . . . Come on, fella . . . sit in a chair . . . *(He takes command, lifts* ALBERT *into a chair.)* Did you ever meet any of her friends, or associates, anybody she knew?

KROLL *(frightened now):* Well, let me think.

FINE: This is what I'm referring to, Albert . . . Do you really have to cloud up like this before you answer that question? Did you ever meet any of her friends?

KROLL: Well, I'm trying to remember!

FINE: Okay, okay. (KROLL *reacts*.) But I said *"any"!* Just in general . . . *a* friend?

KROLL: Well, yes, of course.

FINE: Albert, it's this simple, you are all I've got. If you're not going to level with me, I am out of business. What is it, you afraid of something embarrassing?

KROLL: No—no. I . . . I just . . . *(Breaks off.)*

FINE: What's the problem? You want to find this man, don't you?

KROLL: I heard something drop on piano keys before.

FINE: Yes, I heard it. Probably Douglas; he's dusting for prints.

KROLL: But I don't think Clara had a piano.

FINE *(slight pause):* This is her apartment, isn't it?

KROLL: . . . It seems like it.

FINE: I'm not following you.

KROLL: I'm just wondering, maybe I should wait before I answer any more questions.

FINE: Wait for what?

KROLL: Ah . . . *(Looks confused.)*

FINE: Oh. You mean it might all go 'way.

KROLL: Well, not "go away" exactly, but . . .

FINE: . . . But not be so definite.

KROLL: To be honest . . . I . . . still *(he is groping for the thought)* don't see the necessity. I mean she is not the type of girl who . . . I can't explain what I mean. I mean there was no *necessity* for this.

FINE: I understand.

KROLL *(relieved):* Do you?

FINE: But it's Clara. Why else would you be here, why would you have passed out cold? I think you probably forgot there's a piano here.

KROLL: But everybody loved Clara!

FINE: Except one.

KROLL: Just one in the whole city.

FINE: That's all you need; one makes it a necessity.

KROLL: You know, I do . . . recall now . . . I played on that piano one evening.

FINE: Of course.—Tell me, when you say you did meet friends of hers, how'd that come about?—She ever bring them home?

KROLL: Yes, home. In fact, this last Christmas. A fellow— I'm not trying to hide anything from you . . .

FINE: Good. Was this an associate? A patient?

KROLL: Well, he'd been in prison, but he was out a number of years.

FINE: And . . . what kind of relationship . . . acquaintance or what?

KROLL *(slight pause):* No, I guess it was more than that.

A long pause.

FINE: Yes? (KROLL *gives him a veiled look, then looks at the floor.*) What had he been convicted of, do you know?

KROLL: Murder.

FINE: Who did he murder, did they say?

KROLL *(feeling shame):* A girlfriend.

FINE: Served ten years or something?

KROLL: Something like that, I don't recall.

FINE: What was his name?

KROLL: . . . I'll have to think for a minute.

FINE: Go ahead. *(He resumes going through a file. Then . . .)* She worked at Botsford, you say?

KROLL: Yes.

FINE: She in that riot they had there last summer?

KROLL: Oh, they held her hostage, had a knife to her jugular. *(A laugh)* And when it was over, she went right back in.

FINE: Guess you couldn't talk to her, huh?

KROLL: What can you say?

FINE: Yeah—specially when deep down you were proud of her doing that, right?

KROLL: Well, in a way . . .

FINE: Sure.

> CLARA *is entering with the birdcage, waggling her finger at the bird.*

KROLL: What's the use? She'd always give you the same answer . . . "If my work requires me to be in a place . . . " *(Continues mouthing the words as . . .)*

CLARA: ". . . people somehow know it and they never hassle me."

KROLL (*simultaneously*): "Never hassle me." (*She moves into darkness.—Now he sits staring at the air;* FINE *keeps going through the file.*)

FINE: You're trying to remember that name, right?

KROLL: Name?—Oh, yes, yes. It'll come to me.

FINE: You're in the landscaping business?

KROLL: Not for some years now; my legs, I couldn't take it anymore.

FINE: Oh, you actually did the work?

KROLL: Oh, sure, I did a lot of digging in my time. But pick and shovel gets you in the knees, finally.

FINE: Retired now?

KROLL: No, I'm with Ruggieri Industries.

FINE (*brows knitting*): Ruggieri. Ruggieri Construction?

KROLL: Road building, bridges, heavy stuff. New England.

FINE: Down here too, aren't they?

KROLL: That's Patsy, the brother.

FINE: Right. He had a little trouble there for a while.

KROLL: Ya.

FINE: Right. You're not an easy man to put together, are you? What do you do for Ruggieri?

KROLL: General factotum; I hold down the central office in Poughkeepsie. I'm with Charley, not Patsy.

FINE: Patsy went away for a while, didn't he?

KROLL: But they're completely separate organizations. Charley's never had any trouble.—I mean there's no . . . hit involved here if that's what you . . .

FINE: Uh-huh.—What do you say we really concentrate on this man's name who she brought home? Would your wife remember . . . ?

KROLL: No—no, don't . . . I'll call her if I can't remember . . . I know I'll get it, though.

FINE: Call her yourself if you like.

KROLL *(quickly):* No, I'll do it in a while, if I . . . if I . . . Let's see now . . . *(He seems pressed.)*

FINE: Why'n't we try to reconstruct it.—You live where, in the town, out in the country?

KROLL: In the country. I used to have my nursery next to the house.

FINE: What sort of fella? Jewish, Irish, Italian . . . ?

KROLL *(a slight hesitation):* . . . Hispanic.

FINE: Oh. José? Pablo? Federico? Luis?

KROLL: No.

FINE: Short? Tall?

KROLL: Medium.

FINE: She drive him up?

KROLL: Yeah, they rented a car.

FINE: And what happened, she pulled up in the driveway and got out . . . and did you come out to meet them?

KROLL: I was out; I was on the tractor plowing snow.

FINE: And what?—She kiss you? Shake hands?

KROLL: . . . No. She kissed me.

FINE: And said, "Daddy . . . "? Call you Daddy or Pop?

KROLL: No, Daddy.

FINE: "I want you to meet . . ."? Who?

> KROLL *touches forehead, shaking his head slightly.*

FINE: You know about mental blocks, don't you?—You've been to college, haven't you?

KROLL: No, just high school.

FINE: You seem like a college man.

KROLL: No, I went right to work.

FINE: Generally—you probably know—we block things we're ashamed to remember.

KROLL: I know.

FINE: Things that make us feel guilty, you know what I mean?

KROLL: It'll come to me, I'm still kind of . . . *(Covers his eyes with his fingers.)*

FINE: This animal is digging deeper and deeper into the haystack as we sit here, Albert.

KROLL: I'm trying. I want to help you, it's just hard to keep . . .

FINE: I understand. *(Slight pause)* They stayed the night?

KROLL: Yes.

FINE: And? (KROLL *silent*.) Why'n't you try to relax and let it come? What do you say? (KROLL *looks at him, silent*.) They sleep in the same room?

KROLL: Yes.

FINE *(a synthetic smile):* You could have just told me that, couldn't you?

KROLL: Well, I have. *(Looks down.)*

FINE: But I'm pulling one tooth after another; why string this out? *(A glow of light opens over their heads.)* What do you want me to make out of this, Albert? Are you with me or we going for a walk on flypaper?

"LUIS" *appears overhead and quickly fades out.*

KROLL: Luis.

FINE: Good man. Luis what?

KROLL: But why did I see it . . . like on a screen?

FINE: Maybe the shock . . . Okay now, let's go for the second name. This helps a lot, Albert. Tell me, if you don't mind—how'd you feel about them sleeping together in the house? And, incidentally, how would he have been dressed? Windbreaker? Regular jacket and overcoat . . . ?

KROLL: Windbreaker. Plaid. Like a short mackinaw.

FINE: Good. And you understand if any of these questions are sensitive, it's only to help bring back . . .

KROLL: I understand.

FINE: Where is your wife all this time? She come out to the car?

KROLL *(visualizing):* No, she was in the kitchen cooking dinner.

FINE: So the three of you went inside, right? And Clara says, "Mother? I'd like you to meet Luis . . . " She must have said his second name right then, didn't she? (KROLL *knits his brows, trying . . .*) Okay—how'd your wife react to him? Or wasn't he the first ex-inmate Clara had brought home?

KROLL: No, he was the first.

FINE: And she probably surmised a relationship going on, huh?—What's your wife's name, incidentally?

KROLL: Jean. She did, yes.

FINE: How'd that hit her—this Puerto Rican in a wind-breaker?

KROLL: Jean was a Rockette.

FINE: Excuse me?

KROLL: She'd been dancing in Broadway shows for years when we met—they're accustomed to associating with all kinds of people in show business.

FINE *(skeptically):* Right.

KROLL: . . . I may as well tell you—I had a black company during the war. I spent three years with those men.

FINE: Uh-huh.

KROLL: Although tell you the truth, every once in a while I just about give up on those people, but all I'm saying is . . . you know.

FINE: No. What are you saying?

KROLL: Well, that . . . I've had more than the usual amount of experience with them.

FINE: Tell me: you and Jean—you knew he'd been in prison for murdering his girlfriend?

KROLL: Well, no, they only told about that after dinner.

FINE: I'm curious how that happened to come up.

KROLL: Clara brought it up herself. She was specially proud of his adjustment.

FINE: And you? Can I ask how you felt about that? (KROLL *silent.*) Did you believe it? (KROLL *looks at him.*) . . . The adjustment? . . . I'm just trying to bring back some of your feelings, you see? I mean when she said, "Luis was in prison, Daddy. He murdered his girlfriend." What'd that do to you?

KROLL: I . . . (CLARA *enters, sits facing* KROLL's *profile. She now wears outdoor country clothes, big sweater, slacks.*) . . . felt proud.

FINE: Uh-huh, why?

KROLL: . . . Well, that she was doing some good in the world.

FINE: Right. What good do you mean?

KROLL: Well . . . working with men like that.

FINE: One of whom probably murdered her.

KROLL: Well, yes, but . . . *(Breaks off.)*

FINE: Yes? (KROLL *gropes for a word.*) I'm wondering, Albert—are you guilty because you didn't put your foot down right then and there?

KROLL *(toughening):* I said I was proud of her.

FINE: I'm going to be blunt with you, Albert . . . You mean you're standing there saying good night—is that correct?—while she climbs the stairs to her girlhood room with this convicted killer, and you're full of happiness?

KROLL: I didn't say that . . .

FINE: Then what are you saying? You're not furious and you're not happy. What are you? . . . Forgive me, I'm only trying to help you, but you're blocking this off and I think that's why you can't tell me his name—because you refuse to remember what you were feeling.

KROLL: It's a long time ago . . .

FINE: Two months? But okay, let's relax it, let's just let it come. I'm sorry if I seem like I'm leaning on you, Albert . . .

KROLL: That's okay . . . I'm trying my best . . .

FINE: I figure we're both on the same side, right?

KROLL *(after a pause):* Excuse me saying it, but I would have thought, being Jewish, that you'd have more understanding . . . of this kind of situation. I mean, you're suddenly faced with an underprivileged man like that, you just naturally feel . . .

FINE: Yes, I know what you mean. I used to. I used to have a lot of understanding. But I gave up on it.

KROLL: I see.

FINE: I couldn't deny it; I finally had to face it—I have my limitations; Jewish or not Jewish, I think a man who cuts off a woman's head is a criminal. And if he's been discriminated against and had a bad upbringing, I can only tell you that most of the Puerto Rican people don't become criminals and they have the same background. I used to have a lot of questions about life, but in these last years I'm down to two—what did the guy do, and can I prove it? Whether his mother left him in the same shitty diaper for weeks at a time is not our problem. You agree or not?

KROLL *(pause):* I don't know how to explain . . .

FINE: But you agree with what I just said.

KROLL: Of course, but . . .

FINE: But what, Albert?

KROLL: I can't explain it.

> FINE *goes motionless and light dulls on him.* CLARA *moves now.*

CLARA: He has two things that are a lot like you, Daddy. He's soft and he's strong. And he's overcome so much that we can't even imagine. But it's made him deeper, you see? It's made him love life more . . .

KROLL: I don't understand enough about the mind, darling. How a man can ever kill a woman.

CLARA: But you've killed.

KROLL: In a war. That's a different thing.

CLARA: But you understand rage. You weren't firing from a distance or dropping bombs from a plane . . .

KROLL: But they'd jumped us, Clara. I was fast asleep in the tent and suddenly they were all over me like roaches.

CLARA: You felt that same uncontrollable rage, though . . .

KROLL: It's not the same . . .

CLARA: Yes, it is.—When you grabbed that Japanese and bent him over your knees till you broke his back . . . that was the strength of rage.

KROLL: But this man, with a woman . . .

CLARA: It was his illusion that he was defending his life . . . He'll never have that illusion again, Papa.

KROLL: . . . You know me, darling—I'm always ready to believe the best of anybody . . .

CLARA: I know. But you still don't understand it.

KROLL: No. Before we go to bed, dear . . . unless you don't want any comments . . .

CLARA: Of course I do . . . from you, always.

KROLL: I got the feeling at dinner that you're like a medal he's wearing on his chest. You're like an accomplishment for him.

CLARA: That doesn't have to be a bad thing.

KROLL: No. But is it you he's in love with or the accomplishment? You understand what I mean?

CLARA *(lowered eyes):* Nothing is settled, Papa.

KROLL: God bless you, Clara.

> *She walks into darkness.* FINE *moves.*

FINE: Where would that be, some island? (KROLL *looks at him, uncomprehending.*) That fight in the tent.

KROLL: Oh! Yes, the Philippines. Was I talking? . . . *(Breaks off, points at* FINE. *And still confused about it . . .)* Of course I was, I'm sorry.

FINE *(skeptically):* And you had no rifle? No sidearms?

KROLL: We were all asleep. And then I had to load men into a truck and get them to the aid tent, and I felt this wetness . . . *(a laugh)* . . . and I look down and my whole insides are falling out; I had to drive with one hand! *(Laughs, and holds his belly with his left hand as he mimes steering with the right.)* But I wonder if I should ever have told her that story.

FINE: Made you into a hero.

KROLL: In a way. *(He stares.)*

FINE *(slight pause):* Why, is it a phony story?

KROLL: Heh? No.

FINE *(a moment of hesitation):* You know, Albert, a wound that deep up the belly will stay with a man right into the grave.

KROLL: I know.

FINE: You got a wound like that?

> KROLL, *surprised to be asked, pulls up his shirt and* FINE *looks.* KROLL *puts his shirt back into his trousers.*

FINE: My God.

KROLL: Listen, you won't call my wife, will you? Promise me that.

FINE: How can I promise you? I have to know who he . . .

KROLL: I know it'll come to me, just give me a few minutes. It would be so much worse, a strange voice on the phone . . . You're right, though, I guess I am a little ashamed of one thing. I didn't tell Clara how strongly I felt about this man.

FINE: Of course . . .

KROLL: But by the same token, you see . . . *(a private matter which he hates to speak of)* . . . she was always a serious girl. Never dressed up for boys the way they do . . .

FINE: There'd never been boyfriends?

KROLL: A few, not many. And now she was looking so excited, and all flushed—you know, when she talked about this fellow. I'd never seen that side of her . . .

FINE: So you didn't have the heart to.

KROLL: Yes.

FINE: But Jean knew right away he was dangerous.

KROLL: Pretty much, yes.

FINE: Well, I can see why that's going to be a tough phone call to make.

KROLL: Terrible.

FINE: You mean you actively encouraged Clara.

KROLL: Not *encouraged* . . .

FINE *(impatiently):* Come on, Albert, what's holding you up? I'm not laying judgment on anybody, I just want . . .

KROLL: . . . It's about a year ago now . . . I came down to the city to buy some music . . .

FINE: Records.

KROLL: No. I sing. Churches, even a couple of synagogues. I was a professional after the War, sang in eight musicals, it's how I met Jean.

FINE *(laughs eagerly):* You are something to piece together . . . !

KROLL: I'm not complicated. Anyway, I . . .

FINE: You say synagogues—you're not Jewish, are you?

KROLL: Catholic. But I enjoy the liturgical music.—Where was I? Oh, yes, I had dinner here that evening.—I forgot why I'm telling you this.

FINE: That you're ashamed you didn't put your foot down.

KROLL: Oh. *(Stops.)* I keep feeling I'm falling asleep.

FINE: Well, shocks are funny.—You had dinner here one night.

KROLL: Yes. She had a friend of hers, a social psychologist from Bellevue, I think.

FINE: Man? Woman?

KROLL: Woman.

FINE: Yes?

KROLL: . . . She was a bit older, I think, maybe thirty-five, even forty . . . Not that this necessarily means . . .

FINE: I've been through all the mutations and permutations; I don't make judgments; just try to tell what happened. What happened?

KROLL: Well, it'd gotten late and Clara accompanied her downstairs to her car . . . And after five, ten minutes I started to wonder and went over there to the window and she was . . . standing next to the car talking. *(Sighs.)* And this woman stuck her head out the window. *(Stops.)*

FINE: They kissed?

KROLL: Yes.

FINE: This is what I mean—now you're giving me the story. So in other words . . .

KROLL: I'm not necessarily implying . . .

FINE: What you're telling me, Albert, is that it was such a relief to see her involved with a man . . . even a Puerto Rican murderer wearing a mackinaw, that you . . .

KROLL: I think so . . .

FINE: That's perfectly understandable. You wouldn't recall this woman's name.

KROLL: Her name? ("ELEANOR BALLEN" *flashes overhead*.) Eleanor Ballen.

FINE: Now we're moving!

KROLL: I can't understand why I am seeing it like on a screen . . .

FINE (*making a note*): You are breaking through, you're a hell of a guy . . .

KROLL: He worked at an airport.

FINE: Luis?—which airport?

KROLL: I reached into the car to help with her bag and he took it from me and laughed and said he knew all about handling bags . . . and it came out. But I don't know if he mentioned which one.

FINE: That's all right, keep going.—How about Mercado? Sender? (*To both*, KROLL *gives a negative gesture, staring at his blank memory*.) Let me come at it from a different angle. And try to relax, we're gaining on it.—Am I wrong? I get an impression that you wouldn't want to blame a minority for this . . . on some kind of political grounds?

KROLL: It's not exactly political, but . . . as chairman of the zoning board I've been under terrific pressure to either raise the acreage requirement or lower it. You have to have two and a half acres now . . .

FINE: To build a house.

KROLL: Yes. A lot of them want to raise it to three and even four, and some want to reduce it to one or even less.

FINE: So it's a race problem.

KROLL: Not just race, it's to keep out less affluent families or let them in.

FINE: And where are you on this?

KROLL: We've got to let them in. I don't know what else to support. Or you end up with two societies. In fact, we could easily get sued by the federal government for housing discrimination if we go to four acres. But the feeling runs very hot on both sides . . .

FINE: I can imagine. How hot?

KROLL: Well, for a while there the sheriff told us to move our dining room table away from the picture window. And I've had five or six mailboxes stolen or knocked over, and found a dead rat in the front seat of my car. Some of them get to sounding really crazy.

FINE: You think they could be involved in this?

KROLL: No—no, I can't believe that.

FINE: In other words, if it turned out to be a Puerto Rican, it would be pretty embarrassing for you up there . . . after all you tried to do for them.

> KROLL *simply turns up his palms and shakes his head at the thought of it.*

FINE: What about Menendez? Carillo? Lostados . . . ? (KROLL *indicates "No" and covers his eyes in despair.*) What is it? (KROLL *shakes his head. Then he stares straight ahead at* FINE.) Yes?

KROLL: What time is it now?

FINE: One-o-five.

KROLL *(a pause):* You said that before.

FINE: Make it later, then. Look at yours.

KROLL: I seem to have lost my glasses. *(Searches his pockets.)*

FINE: Albert, listen. (KROLL *goes still.*) You listening? (KROLL *nods.*) You're still guilty about that name, aren't you? (KROLL *looks out front.*) I feel for you. You didn't level with Jean about this lady friend; you didn't put your foot down when you know you never believed that this man was adjusted; and you've gone public in favor of these people coming into the community when you know they're liable to do anything comes into their heads. They are dirty and not responsible and they're going to lower the value of your property, turn the whole area into a slum. You're tied up about this name . . . correct me . . . because you can't stop telling your lies. You're not protecting a name, are you? You'd like this man caught and killed, right? It's not him, it's your lies you can't let go of. It's ten, twenty, thirty years of shit you told your daughter, to the point where she sacrificed her life, for what?—To uphold what you don't believe in yourself.

KROLL: And what do you believe in?

FINE: Me? Greed. Greed and race. Believe it or not, I have never taken an illegitimate nickel, but if you ask what I trust to run the world, it's greed—and that secret little tingle you get when your own kind comes out ahead. The black for the black, and the white for the white. Gentile for Gentile and the Jew for the Jew. Greed and race, Albert, and you'll never go wrong. And, believe me, if you could admit the truth here, I'd have that name in one minute flat.

KROLL: The truth . . .

FINE *(slowly):* You don't owe those people anything. Not then, and especially not now.

    Pause.

KROLL: But your boy . . .

FINE: My boy was shot dead by propaganda that he had some kind of debt to pay. I failed him; I failed to simplify the way it was simplified for me. I took the sergeant's exam three times; I know I got perfect grades three times, but I was one of the kikes, and they finally gave me my stripes out of sheer embarrassment. I was on a par with an Arab bucking for sergeant in the Israeli police department. But it's nothing to be sad about, right? Unless you're going to be way up there looking down at the rest of us down here. But you're working for Ruggieri, you're not way up there, are you?—Not when you're holding down that office for Charley Ruggieri; right? Albert? . . . Albert?

KROLL *(with great difficulty):* That's right.

FINE: I mean the payoffs on those tunnels and highways and bridges—right? You carry the bag, or what? Well, it's none of my business, but in that office you've gotta be one of us, Albert; so how about that name? Clara's gone, kid, there's no reason to carry this on anymore—you're one of us. You admit that to yourself and I'll bet that name comes popping right out.

KROLL: As a matter of fact . . . I don't know what the hell I'm trying to . . . to . . .

FINE: Sure! Get it out, come on—what were you going to say?—And I know how this hurts, kid, but let me tell you a quick one. That day in 1945, remember?—when they first showed those pictures of the piles of bones? Remember that? The bulldozers pushing them into those trenches, those arms and legs sticking up? That's the day I was born again, Albert, and I've never let myself forget it.—"Do it to them before they can do it to you. Period." Now you were saying . . . ?

KROLL *(fear, suddenly):* Sometimes Charley . . . *(Breaks off.)* . . . I don't know why I'm saying this . . .

FINE: Don't hold it, Albert, come on now . . . it's the goods . . . What! Talk to me! Charley Ruggieri?

KROLL *(nods):* Sometimes . . . he goes half crazy trying to figure what to do with himself. He gave his daughter a Miami hotel for her birthday, and a helicopter to his son and two Arabian horses. He flies his jet to London to get some ties. And then the plastic bags.

FINE: What?

KROLL *(with increasing difficulty, but grinning, still amazed):* Gets people together and sit around with plastic bags on their heads till they get high. From the carbon dioxide. Come as close as you can to . . .

FINE: And women?

KROLL: . . . Yes.

FINE: You?

KROLL: A couple times, but I stopped . . .

FINE: Brings on one hell of an erection, doesn't it? Practically rigor mortis.

KROLL: Yes.

FINE *(rapidly, with a driving, contemptuous assurance):* Velazquez? Zuela? Ricon?

> *Negative nods from* KROLL.

FINE: Martinez, Mercado . . .

> *Officer* TIERNEY *enters carrying a record in a cover.*

TIERNEY: This is him, I think; you want it?

FINE *(takes record, looks at cover):* This yours?

KROLL: Oh, long ago, yes. *(Reaches out and is given the cover. Smiles faintly, shakes his head.)* Huh! Yes. *(Hands it back to* FINE.*)* A choral group I had for a while. Many years ago.

FINE *(stares at the record in his hands):* The haircuts in those days! . . . Could I hear it?

> KROLL *shrugs, but seems curious too.*

TIERNEY: Couple of good numbers on it.

FINE *(hesitates, looks at* KROLL, *who seems to be embarrassed):* Go ahead. *(Hands the record to* TIERNEY, *who exits with it.)* Maybe it'll relax you a little; get a new slant, you never know. Got to wait for the Medical Examiner anyway. Can I ask your permission to take a nip of that Scotch over there?

KROLL: Oh, that's okay. (FINE *goes to bottle, pours. Pause*)
That record has got to be at least twenty-five . . .

*A chorus singing "Shenandoah." KROLL's voice, young
and strong, solos in the foreground.*

*TIERNEY enters a moment after KROLL is heard and in-
dicates KROLL to FINE as the soloist.*

KROLL *(hearing his own voice):* Good Lord.

*KROLL is listening, staring front. CLARA enters, a very
young girl now, ribbon in her hair. After a moment . . .*

CLARA: Mama said to ask you.

KROLL: No—no, it's nothing for you to hear; maybe when
you're older.

CLARA: But I want to. Please tell. Daddy? Please!

KROLL *(for a moment he listens to the music which continues behind him):* When the war began they needed officers
so bad they took you without a college degree. When I got
my commission at Benning they sent me over to Missis-
sippi . . . a camp a few miles out of Biloxi.—God, just
listen to that! *(He stares for a moment.)* Most of the officers
were Southerners and I could hardly understand . . .
(Smiles.) . . . you know—what they were saying; or else
they were college guys from the North and they'd be dis-
cussing all these books I never heard of, so I understood
what they were saying but not what they were talking
about. *(A soft laugh)* So it ended up where I'm practically
eating by myself. *(His eyes begin to see, his smile goes.)* The
Army was still completely segregated then, and one day
the Colonel—who was from Alabama, I think—comes into
the mess and asks for a volunteer to take command of a

black company in a new transport battalion—you know, truck drivers and laborers. And of course—nobody wanted a black company. But Grandpa'd always had Negro people working in the nursery and, you know—I'd been around them all my life and always got along with them, and I thought . . . maybe with them I'd have somebody to talk to, so I raised my hand. *(His breathing begins to deepen, his voice on the record strong and young, singing through the air.)* In a couple of months we had a pretty sharp battalion—later in the Pacific MacArthur gave us three citations. But at this time—it was a brutal hot July day and eight or nine of my boys asked if they could go into Biloxi for the afternoon, just to get a beer and walk around. *(Sighs.)* A couple of hours later I get this call that some kind of lynch mob is chasing them through Biloxi and I better come quick. I run into the Colonel's office, but he refused to have anything to do with it. So I said, "Look, I've got hardly any rank, nobody's going to listen to me." But he just walked away. So I strapped on a sidearm and grabbed a jeep and driver from the pool, and we zam down the highway with his foot to the floor, and Biloxi . . . is a madhouse, clumps of people running up and down yelling to each other, people racing around corners with clubs and guns, or down on their hands and knees searching under the porches. Finally I find out a couple of the boys had insulted some white women on the street, and they're going to lynch the whole lot of them. You just couldn't talk to those people, and suddenly I hear this unbelievable roar coming up the avenue and here comes a mob with half a dozen of my guys, some of them already had ropes around their necks. I tried to push through to them, but I couldn't and they're going to hang them then and there. So I jumped up onto the hood of the jeep and took out my .45 and fired it into the air. And they turned around, looking up at me, and I . . . I . . . I didn't know what I was doing by this time, it was like some dream . . . and I yell out . . *(roars).* . . . "I am an officer of the United States Army! Now you untie my men and hand them over to me right now!" *(He glances about before him, almost panting for breath.)* All you could hear was the panting, people trying to catch their breaths. So I called to them, to the boys—"Leroy! Richards! Haley! . . ." And . . . my God, I couldn't believe it . . . one by one they let them out of the crowd. Nobody touched them, and three or four got into the jeep and the rest lay down flat on the hood and some stood on the bumpers and we drove down Main Street and out of the town.—Seems two of them had stopped at a store and seen these great big ladies' hats in the window, and started laughing. Never seen hats like that and it was funny to them, so they fell all over themselves and just then these two women come out of the store and thought they were laughing at *them.* And that's how it started.

CLARA: Oh, Papa . . .

KROLL *(out of his double awareness):* Oh, no. No. No, honey . . . I just didn't have time to think! It was nothing!

CLARA *(kissing his hand):* Papa!

KROLL: No, Clara!—Before I knew it, I was standing there with this gun in my hand . . .

CLARA *(standing):* Oh, my dear Papa . . . !

> *She is moving backward toward the darkness and he is trying to follow . . .*

KROLL: Oh, be careful, darling . . . Oh, my wonderful Clara. *(Straightening, joyfully declaring)* I am so proud of you! *(As she vanishes, his terrified, protesting outcry . . .)* Clara!

A doorbell.

FINE (*to* TIERNEY): Medical Examiner. (TIERNEY *hurries out.*)

"HERNANDEZ" *suddenly blazes up in the air above and vanishes.*

KROLL: Hernandez.

FINE: What!

KROLL: Luis Hernandez. Worked at Kennedy. For Pan American.

> FINE *instantly rushes out.* TIERNEY *appears, carrying the bird in its cage; he pauses for an instant to take in* KROLL, *then goes into the darkness. From the darkness quiet greetings to the doctor—*"Come on in, Doctor, how're you doing?" *etc. The choral recording stops abruptly, the needle lifted off.* KROLL *stares into space, standing erect and calm now.*

C U R T A I N

812.52 Miller, Arthur,
MIL   1915-

        Danger, memory!

    $5.95